The Evolution of Modern Religious Terrorist Organizations

1

Copyright Page

TITLE: The Evolution of Modern Religious Terrorist Organizations

1ST Edition

ISBN: 9798223215325

Table of Contents

The Evolution of Modern Religious Terrorist Organizations

By Roberto Miguel Rodriguez

Chapter 1: Introduction to Modern Terrorist Organizations

Defining Modern Terrorism

In today's world, the rise of modern terrorist organizations has become a pressing concern for scholars, academicians, politicians, legislators, and the public in general. The subchapter "Defining Modern Terrorism" aims to provide a comprehensive understanding of this complex phenomenon within the context of religious extremist organizations, such as Islamic extremism or Christian fundamentalism. By examining the evolution of these groups, we can gain valuable insights into the factors that have contributed to their rise and the unique challenges they pose to global security.

To begin with, it is crucial to establish a clear definition of modern terrorism. Unlike traditional forms of terrorism, modern terrorism is characterized by its transnational nature, sophisticated tactics, and ideological motivations. Rather than focusing solely on political objectives, modern terrorist organizations often draw inspiration from religious ideologies, which can significantly impact their recruitment strategies, operational methods, and overall goals.

When examining the rise of religious extremist organizations, it becomes evident that their ideologies play a pivotal role in shaping their actions. Islamic extremism, for instance, is often fueled by a distorted interpretation of the Quran, which justifies violence as a means to achieve religious purity or political dominance. On the other hand, Christian fundamentalist organizations may draw upon biblical texts to legitimize their acts of violence against perceived threats to their faith.

Understanding the motivations and ideologies behind modern terrorist organizations is essential for formulating effective counterterrorism strategies. By delving into the root causes that drive individuals to join these groups, policymakers and security agencies can develop targeted approaches to prevent radicalization and address the underlying grievances that terrorists exploit.

Moreover, the subchapter will explore the organizational structures and operational methods employed by modern terrorist groups. These organizations have evolved to become highly adaptive and resilient, utilizing advanced technology, social media platforms, and encrypted communication networks. By dissecting their tactics, we can better anticipate and counter their strategies, thereby enhancing global security efforts.

In conclusion, the subchapter "Defining Modern Terrorism" serves as a crucial resource for scholars, academicians, politicians, legislators, and the public interested in understanding the rise of religious extremist organizations. By examining the ideologies, motivations, and operational methods of these groups, we can gain invaluable insights into the complexities of modern terrorism and work towards developing effective strategies to combat this global threat.

Historical Context: Early Terrorist Organizations

Introduction:

Understanding the roots of modern terrorist organizations is crucial in comprehending the rise of religious extremism. This subchapter delves into the historical context of early terrorist organizations, providing a foundation for comprehending the evolution and motivations of contemporary groups. By exploring the origins and ideologies of these early organizations, scholars, academicians, politicians, legislators, and the public in general can gain insights into the development of modern terrorist networks.

Origins of Terrorism:

Terrorism, as a concept, dates back centuries, with early examples found in various regions across the globe. From the Sicarii Zealots in ancient Judea to the Thugs of India, history has witnessed diverse forms of terrorism driven by different ideologies. However, the focus here will be on early terrorist organizations that laid the groundwork for the emergence of religious extremist groups.

Religious Extremism in History:

Religious extremism has played a significant role in shaping terrorist organizations. Examples range from the medieval Assassins, who justified political assassinations through their radical interpretation of Islam, to Christian fundamentalist groups like the Knights Templar, who waged violent campaigns during the Crusades. These early organizations demonstrate the deep historical roots of religiously motivated terrorism.

Motivations and Objectives:

Understanding the motivations and objectives of early terrorist organizations is crucial in comprehending their modern counterparts. Economic, social, political, or religious factors often played a significant role in motivating these groups. The Hashshashin, for instance, sought political power through assassinations, while the Zealots aimed to expel Roman rule from Judea. By studying their ideologies and objectives, we can draw parallels and understand how contemporary religious extremist organizations have evolved.

Impact on Modern Terrorism:

Early terrorist organizations paved the way for the emergence of modern groups driven by religious ideologies. The legacies of these early groups, such as the Thugs' reliance on secrecy and deception, can still be observed in the tactics employed by contemporary organizations. By examining the historical context, we can identify continuities and discontinuities in the strategies, recruitment methods, and propaganda techniques employed by modern terrorist networks.

Conclusion:

The historical context of early terrorist organizations provides scholars, academicians, politicians, legislators, and the public in general with valuable insights into the evolution of modern religious extremist groups. By exploring the origins, motivations, and objectives of these early organizations, we can better understand the rise of religiously motivated terrorism and develop effective strategies to counter its influence. This subchapter serves as a foundational resource for those interested in the niches of modern terrorist organizations and religious extremist organizations driven by ideologies such as Islamic extremism or Christian fundamentalism.

The Shift towards Modern Terrorism

In recent decades, the world has witnessed a significant shift in the nature and tactics of terrorism. This subchapter aims to explore and analyze this shift towards modern terrorism, with a particular focus on the rise of religious extremist organizations. It provides scholars, academicians, politicians, legislators, and the general public with a comprehensive understanding of the factors that have contributed to the evolution of these organizations.

Modern terrorist organizations differ from their predecessors in several key ways. Firstly, they are driven by religious ideologies, such as Islamic extremism or Christian fundamentalism. This religious fervor shapes their objectives, strategies, and justifications for violence. Understanding the motivations behind these religious extremist organizations is crucial for devising effective counterterrorism strategies.

Religious extremist organizations have emerged as a dominant force in contemporary terrorism due to various factors. One significant factor is the globalization of information and communication technologies, which has facilitated the rapid dissemination of extremist ideologies. The internet, social media platforms, and encrypted messaging applications have become breeding grounds for radicalization and recruitment. This subchapter explores the role of these technologies in the rise of modern terrorism and the challenges they pose to counterterrorism efforts.

Another factor contributing to the shift towards modern terrorism is the changing geopolitical landscape. The decline of state authority, the rise of failed states, and the erosion of traditional power structures have created fertile ground for extremist groups to thrive. They exploit political instability, ethnic tensions, and social grievances to gain support and establish their presence. Examining these underlying factors is essential for understanding the root causes of terrorism and developing effective prevention strategies.

Furthermore, the subchapter delves into the tactics employed by modern terrorist organizations. Unlike their predecessors, these groups have demonstrated a remarkable ability to adapt and innovate. They have embraced asymmetrical warfare, using suicide bombings, kidnappings, and cyber-attacks to instill fear and achieve their objectives. Understanding these tactics is crucial for enhancing security measures and safeguarding against future attacks.

Ultimately, comprehending the shift towards modern terrorism and religious extremist organizations is vital for policymakers, legislators, and the wider public. This subchapter provides a comprehensive analysis of the evolving landscape of terrorism, shedding light on the complex interplay of religious ideologies, geopolitical dynamics, and technological advancements. By understanding these factors, we can develop more effective strategies to counter the threat posed by modern terrorist organizations and promote peace and stability in our societies.

Factors Contributing to the Rise of Modern Terrorist Organizations

Introduction:

The rise of modern terrorist organizations, particularly those driven by religious extremism, is a complex phenomenon that demands careful analysis and understanding. This subchapter aims to delve into the various factors that have contributed to the emergence and growth of these organizations. By examining social, political, and economic factors, we can gain insight into the root causes of religious extremist terrorism and explore potential strategies to counter its influence.

Social Factors:

A major factor contributing to the rise of modern terrorist organizations is the existence of social grievances and marginalization. Many individuals who join these organizations feel excluded from mainstream society, experiencing discrimination, poverty, and lack of opportunities. Often, religious extremist groups offer a sense of belonging, purpose, and empowerment, attracting individuals who seek revenge or a voice against perceived injustices. Understanding and addressing these social grievances is crucial to mitigating the appeal of these organizations.

Political Factors:

Political instability and governance failures have also played a significant role in the rise of modern terrorist organizations. Weak or corrupt governments, lack of accountability, and repressive policies can create an environment conducive to the growth of extremist ideologies. Additionally, geopolitical conflicts, such as foreign military interventions or territorial disputes, can fuel resentment and provide fertile ground for recruitment. It is essential for policymakers to prioritize good governance, inclusivity, and conflict resolution to undermine the appeal of extremist ideologies.

Economic Factors:

Economic factors, including poverty, unemployment, and unequal distribution of resources, contribute to the vulnerability of individuals susceptible to radicalization. Economic hardships can make individuals more susceptible to recruitment, as terrorist organizations often promise financial stability and support to their members and their families. Addressing economic disparities and promoting inclusive economic growth is vital in countering the appeal of these organizations.

Conclusion:

Understanding the factors contributing to the rise of modern terrorist organizations is crucial in developing effective strategies to counter their influence. By comprehending the social, political, and economic dynamics that fuel religious extremist ideologies, policymakers, scholars, and the public can work towards creating a more inclusive society, enhancing governance, and promoting economic development. By addressing these underlying factors, we can help prevent the growth of terrorist organizations and mitigate the threat they pose to global peace and security.

Purpose and Structure of the Book

Introduction:

"The Evolution of Modern Terrorist Organizations: Understanding the Rise of Religious Extremism" aims to provide scholars, academicians, politicians, legislators, and the general public with a comprehensive understanding of the emergence and growth of modern terrorist organizations driven by religious ideologies. This subchapter will outline the purpose and structure of the book, giving readers a clear roadmap of what to expect.

Chapter Overview:

1. Unveiling the Rise of Modern Terrorist Organizations:

This chapter sets the stage by providing an overview of the historical context and factors that led to the rise of modern terrorist organizations. It delves into the global socio-political landscape, highlighting the critical events and ideological shifts that have contributed to the growth of religious extremism.

2. Understanding Religious Extremist Organizations:

This section explores the mindset and motivations of religious extremist organizations. It examines the key characteristics that distinguish them from other terrorist groups, such as their religious ideologies and the role of charismatic leaders. Detailed case studies will shed light on the inner workings of prominent organizations like Al-Qaeda and ISIS.

3. Analyzing the Root Causes of Religious Extremism:

To fully comprehend the rise of religious extremism, this chapter delves into the underlying factors that fuel its growth. It explores socio-economic disparities, political grievances, and the impact of foreign interventions, providing a nuanced understanding of the root causes that drive individuals towards extremism.

4. The Role of Religion in Modern Terrorism:

This section examines the complex relationship between religion and terrorism. It analyzes how religious texts and interpretations can be manipulated to justify violence and radical behavior. By examining both Islamic extremism and Christian fundamentalism, this chapter aims to dispel misconceptions and foster a more informed dialogue.

5. Counterterrorism Strategies and Future Prospects:

The final chapter explores effective counterterrorism strategies, highlighting successful initiatives and lessons learned from past experiences. It also offers forward-thinking perspectives on the future of religious extremist organizations, considering potential trends and challenges that lie ahead.

Conclusion:

"The Evolution of Modern Terrorist Organizations: Understanding the Rise of Religious Extremism" provides a comprehensive analysis of the key aspects surrounding modern terrorist organizations driven by religious ideologies. By examining the historical, socio-political, and religious factors contributing to their rise, this book aims to equip scholars, academicians, politicians, legislators, and the general public with a deeper understanding of these complex phenomena. It is our hope that this knowledge will foster informed discussions, inspire effective counterterrorism strategies, and ultimately contribute to a safer and more peaceful world.

Chapter 2: Understanding Religious Extremist Organizations

Definition and Characteristics of Religious Extremism

Religious extremism, a phenomenon that has gained significant attention in recent years, refers to the rigid interpretation and application of religious doctrines that leads individuals or groups to engage in violent and radical actions. This subchapter aims to provide a comprehensive understanding of religious extremism, its defining characteristics, and its implications for modern terrorist organizations.

At its core, religious extremism is driven by a fervent and unwavering belief in the supremacy and exclusivity of one's religious ideology. This ideology often rejects any form of compromise, dialogue, or coexistence with other belief systems, labeling them as heretical or infidel. Such extremism can be found in various religious contexts, including Islamic extremism, Christian fundamentalism, and Hindu nationalism, among others.

One of the key characteristics of religious extremism is the intentional distortion of religious texts and teachings to justify violence and aggression. Extremists selectively interpret religious scriptures, taking passages out of context and manipulating them to suit their ideological goals. They often glorify martyrdom and believe that violence is a legitimate means to achieve their religious objectives.

Furthermore, religious extremists exhibit a strong sense of identity and belonging to their religious community, often perceiving themselves as the righteous defenders of their faith. They see the world as a battleground between good and evil, with their religious group representing the forces of righteousness. This mindset fosters a strong sense of us-versus-them mentality, leading to the dehumanization and demonization of those who do not adhere to their religious beliefs.

In addition, religious extremism is often characterized by a rejection of modernity and secular values. Extremist groups may resist social, political, and cultural changes, perceiving them as threats to their religious identity and traditions. This resistance often manifests in a desire to establish a theocratic state governed by strict religious laws and practices.

The implications of religious extremism are far-reaching and complex. It poses a significant threat to global peace and security, as extremist organizations resort to acts of terrorism to advance their religious agendas. The rise of modern terrorist organizations, such as Al-Qaeda, ISIS, Boko Haram, and the Taliban, exemplify the dangerous consequences of religious extremism.

In conclusion, religious extremism is characterized by a rigid and uncompromising interpretation of religious doctrines, intentional distortion of religious texts, strong group identity, and rejection of modernity. Understanding these defining characteristics is crucial for scholars, academicians, politicians, legislators, and the general public, as it allows for a deeper understanding of the rise and evolution of modern terrorist organizations driven by religious ideologies. By comprehending the roots and manifestations of religious extremism, we can develop effective strategies to counter its influence and promote peaceful coexistence among diverse religious communities.

Historical Background of Religious Extremism

Religious extremism is not a new phenomenon; it has deep roots in history and has influenced the development of modern terrorist organizations. Understanding the historical background of religious extremism is crucial in comprehending the rise of these organizations and their ideologies.

The origins of religious extremism can be traced back to ancient times when religious beliefs played a central role in society. Throughout history, various religious groups have emerged, holding radical interpretations of their faith and advocating for extreme measures to enforce their beliefs. These groups often view the world through a religious lens, perceiving themselves as the chosen ones and struggling against those who disagree with their ideology.

One significant historical event that influenced the rise of religious extremism is the Crusades. During the medieval period, Christian armies embarked on a series of military expeditions to reclaim the Holy Land from Muslim control. This period witnessed the emergence of religiously motivated violence on a large scale, as both Christians and Muslims committed atrocities in the name of their faith. The impact of the Crusades on interfaith relations and the perpetuation of religious conflict cannot be underestimated.

In more recent history, the 20th century saw the rise of Islamic extremism, particularly with the establishment of political entities such as the Muslim Brotherhood in Egypt and the Islamic Revolution in Iran. These movements sought to establish Islamic states governed by strict interpretations of religious laws. Their ideologies merged political aspirations with religious convictions, resulting in the birth of modern terrorist organizations like Al-Qaeda and ISIS.

Similarly, Christian fundamentalism has also played a role in shaping religious extremism. In the United States, for example, Christian extremist groups have emerged, advocating for the imposition of religious laws and resisting social changes that they perceive as contrary to their religious values. These groups have been involved in acts of violence and domestic terrorism, highlighting the dangerous consequences of religious extremism.

Understanding the historical context of religious extremism is essential for scholars, academicians, politicians, legislators, and the general public. By examining the roots of these ideologies, we can gain insights into the motivations and tactics of modern terrorist organizations. Moreover, it enables us to develop effective strategies to counter religious extremism and promote tolerance and understanding among different faith communities.

In conclusion, the historical background of religious extremism provides valuable insights into the origins and development of modern terrorist organizations. By studying the Crusades, the rise of Islamic extremism, and the emergence of Christian fundamentalism, we can better understand the complex dynamics of religiously motivated violence. This knowledge is crucial for scholars, academicians, politicians, legislators, and the public in general to address the challenges posed by religious extremist organizations and work towards a more peaceful and inclusive world.

Religious Ideologies and their Influence on Terrorism

Introduction:

Religious ideologies have played a significant role in shaping the tactics, motivations, and recruitment strategies of modern terrorist organizations. This subchapter explores the nexus between religious extremism and terrorism, focusing on how these ideologies influence the rise of violent organizations driven by Islamic extremism or Christian fundamentalism. By understanding the underlying religious ideologies, scholars, academicians, politicians, legislators, and the public in general can gain valuable insights into the dynamics of modern terrorist organizations and devise effective countermeasures.

Understanding Religious Ideologies:

Religious ideologies provide a framework for interpreting the world and offer a sense of identity, purpose, and belonging. However, when taken to an extreme, they can foster a mindset that justifies violence and terrorism. This subchapter delves into the core beliefs and interpretations of Islamic extremism and Christian fundamentalism, highlighting how these ideologies can be manipulated by terrorist organizations to legitimize their actions.

Recruitment and Radicalization:

The influence of religious ideologies on terrorism is particularly evident in the recruitment and radicalization processes. Modern terrorist organizations exploit religious narratives and symbols to attract vulnerable individuals seeking meaning or redemption. By examining case studies and real-life examples, this subchapter sheds light on the mechanisms employed by these organizations to indoctrinate individuals and transform them into radicalized extremists.

Motivations and Tactics:

Religious ideologies provide terrorists with a moral justification for their actions, often framing violence as an act of divine duty or a means to an end. This subchapter explores the motivations behind religiously driven terrorist acts, such as the establishment of an Islamic caliphate or the protection of Christian values. Additionally, it addresses the tactics employed by these organizations, including suicide bombings, mass shootings, and attacks on symbolic targets.

Challenges and Countermeasures:

Understanding the influence of religious ideologies on terrorism is crucial for devising effective countermeasures. This subchapter examines the challenges faced by governments, security agencies, and policymakers in combating religious extremist organizations. It also explores strategies for countering the appeal of these ideologies, including promoting religious tolerance, supporting moderate voices, and addressing socio-economic grievances that contribute to radicalization.

Conclusion:

Religious ideologies have become a driving force behind the rise of modern terrorist organizations. By comprehending the influence of religious extremism on terrorism, scholars, academicians, politicians, legislators, and the public can develop a nuanced understanding of these organizations and work towards mitigating their impact. Only by tackling the root causes of religious extremism and addressing the grievances that fuel it can societies hope to effectively combat the rise of violence perpetrated in the name of religion.

Factors that Drive Religious Extremist Organizations

Religious extremist organizations have become a significant global concern in recent times. This subchapter aims to delve into the factors that drive these organizations, shedding light on the intricate web of ideologies, motivations, and circumstances that contribute to their rise and growth. By understanding these factors, scholars, academicians, politicians, legislators, and the general public can gain valuable insights into the evolution of modern terrorist organizations and the rise of religious extremism.

One of the primary driving factors behind religious extremist organizations is the profound influence of religious ideologies. These organizations are often rooted in religious beliefs that they interpret in an extreme and radical manner. Islamic extremism and Christian fundamentalism are two prominent examples of religious ideologies that have fueled the growth of terrorist organizations. The interpretation of religious texts, historical events, and societal grievances can provide a distorted framework that justifies violence, creating an environment conducive to recruitment and radicalization.

Socio-political factors also play a crucial role in driving religious extremist organizations. Economic disparities, political instability, marginalization, and the erosion of traditional cultural values can create fertile ground for extremist ideologies to take root. These organizations often exploit grievances arising from real or perceived injustices, offering a sense of purpose and identity to individuals who feel marginalized or disenfranchised.

The role of technology and globalization cannot be overlooked when examining the factors that drive religious extremist organizations. The internet and social media platforms have revolutionized the way these organizations recruit, radicalize, and communicate. Online platforms provide a global reach, allowing extremist ideologies to transcend borders and attract individuals from diverse backgrounds. The rapid dissemination of propaganda and the ability to connect with like-minded individuals have significantly facilitated the growth of such organizations.

Furthermore, external geopolitical factors, such as foreign interventions and conflicts, also contribute to the rise of religious extremist organizations. These organizations often emerge or gain strength in regions plagued by instability, such as the Middle East or parts of Africa. The presence of foreign military forces, political interventions, and protracted conflicts can create a breeding ground for radicalization as individuals seek to resist perceived external aggression or defend their religious beliefs.

In conclusion, the factors driving religious extremist organizations are complex and multifaceted. Religious ideologies, socio-political factors, technological advancements, and geopolitical dynamics all contribute to their rise and growth. Understanding these factors is crucial for scholars, academicians, politicians, legislators, and the general public to effectively combat the menace of modern terrorist organizations driven by religious extremism. By addressing the root causes and underlying factors, society can work towards promoting peace, tolerance, and understanding.

Comparison of Religious Extremism with Secular Terrorism

Introduction:

In recent decades, the rise of religious extremism has become a significant concern for the global community. This subchapter aims to shed light on the comparison between religious extremism and secular terrorism, providing scholars, academicians, politicians, legislators, and the public in general with a comprehensive understanding of this evolving threat. By examining modern terrorist organizations driven by religious ideologies, such as Islamic extremism or Christian fundamentalism, we can discern key similarities and differences between these groups and their secular counterparts.

Religious Extremism: A Catalyst for Terrorism:

Religious extremist organizations derive their motivation from deeply rooted ideological beliefs. They seek to establish a society governed by rigid religious principles, often disregarding the rights and freedoms of others. These groups, such as ISIS or Boko Haram, exploit religion as a powerful tool to recruit, indoctrinate, and radicalize individuals, ultimately leading to acts of violence in pursuit of their objectives.

Secular Terrorism: A Quest for Political Change:

Contrasting religious extremism, secular terrorism emerges from political and social grievances. These organizations, like the IRA or the Red Army Faction, employ violence to challenge existing power structures and promote their political agenda. While religious extremists aim to establish a theocracy, secular terrorists typically seek to overthrow a government or establish a new social order based on their ideological principles.

Similarities and Differences:

Despite their distinct motivations, religious extremism and secular terrorism share certain characteristics. Both exhibit a willingness to use violence to achieve their objectives, posing a threat to national and international security. Moreover, both types of organizations often operate within clandestine networks, employing recruitment strategies and propaganda to expand their influence.

However, one key difference lies in the role of religion. Religious extremist organizations use religious texts and doctrines to justify their acts of violence, perceiving their actions as divinely ordained. On the other hand, secular terrorist organizations rarely rely on religious ideology to legitimize their violence. Their motivations stem from political, social, or economic factors, making their actions appear more pragmatic and strategic.

Conclusion:

Understanding the similarities and differences between religious extremism and secular terrorism is crucial for formulating effective counter-terrorism strategies. By recognizing the underlying motivations and ideologies that drive these organizations, policymakers, legislators, and scholars can develop comprehensive approaches to mitigate the threat posed by modern terrorist organizations. By addressing the root causes and adopting a multi-faceted approach, we can strive towards a safer and more peaceful future.

Chapter 3: Case Studies of Modern Terrorist Organizations

Al-Qaeda: The Birth of Global Jihadism

The birth of Al-Qaeda marked a turning point in the evolution of modern terrorist organizations. This subchapter delves into the origins and rise of Al-Qaeda, shedding light on its early days, ideology, and its impact on global jihadism.

Al-Qaeda emerged in the late 1980s as a result of the Soviet-Afghan War, when Arab fighters, including Osama bin Laden, flocked to Afghanistan to support the mujahideen against Soviet forces. It was during this time that bin Laden, a wealthy Saudi Arabian, established strong connections and developed his radical Islamist ideology. Drawing inspiration from the teachings of Sayyid Qutb and Abdullah Azzam, bin Laden envisioned a global jihad against perceived enemies of Islam.

The subchapter explores the ideological underpinnings of Al-Qaeda, examining how its worldview was shaped by a combination of religious extremism, anti-Western sentiments, and grievances against perceived Western imperialism. It highlights the key tenets of Al-Qaeda's ideology, including the call for a strict interpretation of Islamic law, the establishment of a caliphate, and the duty to wage jihad against non-believers.

Furthermore, the subchapter delves into the operational structure and tactics employed by Al-Qaeda. It analyzes the group's decentralized nature, with regional affiliates and cells operating independently but united by a common ideology and shared objectives. It also examines Al-Qaeda's use of propaganda, recruitment strategies, and the role of the Internet in disseminating its extremist ideology.

The impact of Al-Qaeda on global jihadism is a central theme of this subchapter. It explores the influence of Al-Qaeda on subsequent terrorist organizations, such as ISIS, and the spread of its ideology beyond the Middle East. Additionally, it addresses the role of Al-Qaeda in inspiring and carrying out major attacks, including the 9/11 attacks in the United States, Madrid train bombings, and London bombings, among others.

Finally, this subchapter examines the response of governments and international organizations to the rise of Al-Qaeda. It analyzes the evolution of counterterrorism strategies, the challenges faced in combating a decentralized and transnational organization, and the role of military interventions in countering global jihadism.

Overall, this subchapter provides a comprehensive overview of Al-Qaeda's birth, ideology, operational tactics, and its impact on global jihadism. It caters to scholars, academicians, politicians, legislators, and the public in general with an interest in understanding modern terrorist organizations and the rise of religious extremism. It also appeals to individuals interested in exploring the intersection between religious ideologies and terrorism.

Genesis of Al-Qaeda

The birth and evolution of Al-Qaeda represent a critical chapter in the history of modern terrorist organizations and religious extremism. Understanding the genesis of this notorious group is essential for scholars, academicians, politicians, legislators, and the general public who seek to comprehend the rise of religiously motivated terrorism. This subchapter delves into the origins of Al-Qaeda, shedding light on the factors that contributed to its formation and subsequent growth.

Al-Qaeda emerged in the late 1980s, during the Soviet-Afghan War. The conflict provided a fertile ground for the convergence of various jihadist factions, united by their opposition to the Soviet occupation of Afghanistan. Osama bin Laden, a wealthy Saudi Arabian, played a pivotal role in the formation of Al-Qaeda. He leveraged his resources, networks, and charismatic leadership to unite disparate groups under a common cause. Bin Laden's vision extended beyond Afghanistan, envisioning a global jihad against perceived enemies of Islam.

The ideological foundation of Al-Qaeda can be traced back to the teachings of radical Islamic scholars such as Sayyid Qutb and Abdullah Azzam. These thinkers propagated a militant interpretation of Islam, calling for the establishment of a global Islamic caliphate and the rejection of Western influence. Bin Laden absorbed these ideas and incorporated them into his worldview, which became the ideological basis for Al-Qaeda's actions.

One pivotal event in Al-Qaeda's genesis was the 1996 declaration of a fatwa by bin Laden, proclaiming a holy war against the United States and its allies. This marked a turning point in the group's evolution, as it shifted its focus from regional conflicts to global jihad. The subsequent attacks on American embassies in Kenya and Tanzania in 1998, and the devastating 9/11 attacks in 2001, catapulted Al-Qaeda to the forefront of international terrorism.

The genesis of Al-Qaeda was also facilitated by a range of socio-political factors. These included the power vacuum left by the Soviet withdrawal from Afghanistan, the absence of effective governance in certain regions, and grievances stemming from perceived Western interference in Muslim lands. Additionally, the emergence of new communication technologies, such as the internet, enabled Al-Qaeda to disseminate its messages and recruit followers globally, further fueling its growth.

In conclusion, the genesis of Al-Qaeda can be attributed to a complex interplay of historical, ideological, and socio-political factors. Understanding these origins is crucial for comprehending the rise of religiously motivated terrorist organizations in the modern world. By examining Al-Qaeda's evolution, scholars, academicians, politicians, legislators, and the general public can gain valuable insights into the broader phenomenon of religious extremism, which extends beyond Islam to encompass other religious ideologies as well.

Ideological Beliefs and Goals of Al-Qaeda

Introduction:

Al-Qaeda, a notorious terrorist organization, has gained global attention due to its brutal acts of violence and its extremist ideology. This subchapter aims to delve into the ideological beliefs and goals that drive the actions of Al-Qaeda. By understanding the motivations behind their actions, scholars, academicians, politicians, legislators, and the public in general can gain valuable insights into the rise of religious extremism and the evolution of modern terrorist organizations.

Religious Extremism as a Catalyst:

Al-Qaeda's ideology is rooted in Islamic extremism, which serves as a primary motivator for its actions. The organization believes in the establishment of a global Islamic caliphate governed by Sharia law. This religious fervor drives Al-Qaeda's relentless pursuit of its goals, as it perceives itself as a vanguard for purifying Islam from perceived corruption and Western influence.

The Jihadist Narrative:

Al-Qaeda's ideological beliefs are manifested through its narrative of jihad, commonly known as holy war. According to their interpretation, jihad is a duty imposed upon all Muslims to defend and propagate Islam. Al-Qaeda justifies its acts of violence as a means to protect and expand the Muslim ummah (community) by targeting perceived enemies, including Western nations, non-Muslims, and apostate regimes in the Muslim world.

Global Aspirations and Strategy:

Al-Qaeda's ultimate goal is to overthrow existing governments in Muslim-majority countries and replace them with Islamic states that adhere strictly to their interpretation of Sharia law. The organization aims to expel Western influence from Muslim lands and establish a united front against perceived enemies of Islam. Al-Qaeda's strategy includes conducting high-profile attacks on symbolic targets, such as the 9/11 attacks in the United States, to provoke a violent clash between Islam and the West, thereby mobilizing Muslims worldwide to join their cause.

Recruitment and Radicalization:

Understanding Al-Qaeda's ideological beliefs and goals is crucial in combating their influence. Their narrative of jihad, combined with a sense of injustice and a perception of global Muslim suffering, serves as a powerful recruitment tool, particularly among marginalized and disaffected individuals. Addressing the root causes of radicalization, including socioeconomic grievances and political oppression, is essential to counter Al-Qaeda's appeal and prevent individuals from being drawn into their ranks.

Conclusion:

Exploring the ideological beliefs and goals of Al-Qaeda provides valuable insights into the rise of religious extremism and the evolution of modern terrorist organizations. Recognizing the power of religious narratives, understanding the motivations behind their actions, and addressing the root causes of radicalization are key steps in countering their influence. By analyzing Al-Qaeda's ideology, scholars, academicians, politicians, legislators, and the public can contribute to the development of effective strategies to combat terrorism, protect global security, and promote peace and understanding among different religious communities.

Tactics and Strategies Employed by Al-Qaeda

Introduction:

The subchapter "Tactics and Strategies Employed by Al-Qaeda" delves into the operational methods of one of the most notorious modern terrorist organizations. Addressed to scholars, academicians, politicians, legislators, and the general public, this section aims to provide a comprehensive understanding of Al-Qaeda's tactics and strategies. By examining the rise of religious extremism, particularly Islamic extremism, this subchapter also offers insights into the broader context in which Al-Qaeda operates.

Understanding Al-Qaeda's Tactics:

Al-Qaeda has demonstrated a multifaceted approach to achieving its objectives, combining both traditional and unconventional tactics. One of its primary tactics is the use of suicide bombings, which have proven devastatingly effective in creating fear and instability. Al-Qaeda also employs guerrilla warfare, utilizing hit-and-run attacks and ambushes, often targeting military and government installations. Furthermore, the organization capitalizes on propaganda and media manipulation to inspire and recruit individuals to its cause.

Strategies of Al-Qaeda:

Al-Qaeda's strategies are centered around four key objectives: establishing a global caliphate, conducting asymmetrical warfare against perceived enemies, destabilizing nations, and promoting radical ideologies. To achieve these goals, the organization has adopted several strategies. Firstly, it engages in asymmetric warfare, using small, decentralized cells to strike at high-value targets while minimizing its own vulnerabilities. Secondly, Al-Qaeda exploits weak governance and political instability in regions where it operates, aiming to create power vacuums that can be filled with its own extremist ideologies.

Additionally, Al-Qaeda pursues a global strategy, aiming to spread its influence beyond its traditional strongholds. It forms alliances and collaborates with other extremist organizations, such as the Taliban and Boko Haram, sharing resources, knowledge, and operational capabilities. Lastly, Al-Qaeda capitalizes on modern technology, particularly the internet, to disseminate its propaganda, radicalize individuals, and coordinate attacks.

Implications and Countermeasures:

Understanding Al-Qaeda's tactics and strategies is crucial for developing effective countermeasures against this and other religious extremist organizations. Policymakers and legislators must prioritize intelligence gathering, international cooperation, and law enforcement efforts to dismantle and disrupt the organization's networks. Additionally, countering extremist ideologies through education, community engagement, and promoting moderate interpretations of religion is essential in preventing the radicalization of vulnerable individuals.

Conclusion:

This subchapter has shed light on the tactics and strategies employed by Al-Qaeda, a modern terrorist organization driven by religious extremism. By examining their operational methods, we gain a deeper understanding of the challenges posed by such organizations. Armed with this knowledge, scholars, academicians, politicians, legislators, and the general public can contribute to the development of effective strategies that address the rise of religious extremism and ensure a safer world for all.

Impact and Legacy of Al-Qaeda

Introduction:

The emergence of Al-Qaeda marked a turning point in the history of modern terrorist organizations. Its impact on global security and the legacy it left behind cannot be underestimated. This subchapter delves into the profound consequences of Al-Qaeda's activities and the lasting effects it has had on international relations, counterterrorism efforts, and the rise of religious extremism.

1. Shaping Global Security:

Al-Qaeda's attacks on September 11, 2001, forever changed the landscape of global security. The devastating strikes on the World Trade Center and the Pentagon exposed the vulnerability of even the most powerful nations. The event prompted a paradigm shift in counterterrorism strategies, leading to the establishment of new security measures, intelligence sharing networks, and the reevaluation of international alliances.

2. Inspiring Copycat Attacks:

Al-Qaeda's successful execution of large-scale attacks inspired and emboldened other extremist groups worldwide. Its media-savvy approach, including the dissemination of propaganda videos and recruitment materials, influenced subsequent organizations such as ISIS. The legacy of Al-Qaeda's tactics continues to reverberate through the actions of these groups, prolonging the threat of global terrorism.

3. Globalization of Jihadist Networks:

Al-Qaeda's influence extended beyond its immediate structures. Through its global jihadist network, it fostered connections with like-minded individuals and groups, enabling the spread of its extremist ideology and operational expertise. This globalization of jihadist networks facilitated the expansion of religious extremist organizations worldwide, contributing to the rise of other groups sharing a similar radical Islamic ideology.

4. Heightened Religious Extremism:

Al-Qaeda's adoption of a distorted interpretation of Islam to justify its violent actions had a profound impact on religious extremism. It sowed the seeds of discontent and polarization within Muslim communities, leading to an increase in radicalization. The legacy of Al-Qaeda continues to fuel religious extremist organizations, such as Islamic State, Boko Haram, and Al-Shabaab, which operate in different parts of the world.

5. The War on Terror:

The U.S. response to the 9/11 attacks, commonly known as the "War on Terror," shaped global politics and security policies. The invasion of Afghanistan and subsequent military interventions in Iraq and other regions highlighted the challenges faced by nations combating terrorism. The legacy of Al-Qaeda's actions persists in ongoing conflicts and the complex dynamics of counterterrorism efforts worldwide.

Conclusion:

The impact and legacy of Al-Qaeda are far-reaching and continue to shape the contemporary security landscape. Its attacks not only transformed global security practices but also inspired the rise of other religious extremist organizations. Recognizing and understanding these consequences are vital for scholars, academicians, politicians, legislators, and the general public. Only through a comprehensive understanding of Al-Qaeda's impact can we effectively address the ongoing challenges posed by modern terrorist organizations and religious extremism.

ISIS: The Emergence of the Caliphate

The rise of the Islamic State of Iraq and Syria (ISIS) and the subsequent establishment of the self-proclaimed Caliphate in 2014 marks a significant turning point in the evolution of modern terrorist organizations. This subchapter delves into the factors that contributed to the emergence of this highly influential and brutal group, providing insight into the dynamics of modern terrorist organizations driven by religious extremism.

The roots of ISIS can be traced back to the aftermath of the U.S. invasion of Iraq in 2003, which created a power vacuum and sectarian tensions within the country. Exploiting these divisions, Abu Musab al-Zarqawi, the founder of ISIS's predecessor, al-Qaeda in Iraq, sought to establish an Islamic state governed by strict Sharia law. Al-Zarqawi's death in 2006 did little to hinder the group's progress, as it continued to recruit and expand its operations under the leadership of Abu Bakr al-Baghdadi.

One of the key factors that contributed to the success of ISIS was its adept use of social media and online platforms. Unlike previous terrorist organizations, ISIS effectively utilized the internet to disseminate its propaganda, recruit foreign fighters, and inspire lone-wolf attacks across the globe. This unprecedented online presence allowed them to establish a global network of sympathizers and supporters, further bolstering their ranks and influence.

The proclamation of the Caliphate by al-Baghdadi in 2014 was a significant milestone for ISIS. It aimed to restore the Islamic caliphate, a political and religious institution that had been abolished nearly a century ago. The declaration not only galvanized supporters but also attracted disaffected individuals from various backgrounds, many of whom were drawn to the allure of a utopian Islamic state.

The brutality exhibited by ISIS, including mass executions, beheadings, and the enslavement of women, shocked the world. These acts served a dual purpose for the group: they instilled fear among their enemies and attracted individuals who were already predisposed to violence and radical ideologies. This created a self-sustaining cycle of violence and recruitment, further solidifying the influence of the Caliphate.

Understanding the emergence of the ISIS Caliphate requires a comprehensive analysis of the political, social, and religious factors that contributed to its rise. By examining the strategies employed by this group, scholars, academicians, politicians, and legislators can gain valuable insights into the broader phenomenon of modern terrorist organizations driven by religious extremism. Such understanding is crucial in formulating effective counterterrorism policies and preventing the spread of religious extremist ideologies.

Rise of ISIS and the Collapse of Al-Qaeda's Influence

In the ever-evolving landscape of modern terrorist organizations, the rise of ISIS and the subsequent collapse of Al-Qaeda's influence have been pivotal moments that have shaped the trajectory of global terrorism. This subchapter aims to dissect and analyze these significant events, offering insights into the factors that led to the emergence of ISIS and its subsequent impact on the influence of Al-Qaeda. It is an essential read for scholars, academicians, politicians, legislators, and the general public interested in understanding the rise of religious extremism, particularly within the context of modern terrorist organizations.

The subchapter begins by examining the historical context that laid the groundwork for the rise of ISIS. It delves into the power vacuum created by the United States' invasion of Iraq in 2003, the subsequent dismantling of Saddam Hussein's regime, and the alienation of Sunni Muslims in the country. These factors provided fertile ground for the growth of a new extremist group that capitalized on the grievances and disillusionment of marginalized individuals.

The content then explores the ideological underpinnings of ISIS, examining its interpretation of Islamic extremism and its ambition to establish a Caliphate. It delves into the group's sophisticated propaganda machinery, its use of social media, and its ability to attract and radicalize individuals from around the world. By understanding these elements, scholars and academicians can gain valuable insights into the tactics and strategies employed by religious extremist organizations.

Furthermore, the subchapter analyzes the impact of ISIS on Al-Qaeda's influence. It examines the rivalry between the two groups, the ideological differences that emerged, and the subsequent decline of Al-Qaeda's prominence. Through a comparative analysis, it becomes evident that ISIS's ability to capture global attention, control territory, and carry out high-profile attacks diminished Al-Qaeda's appeal and influence among potential recruits.

The subchapter concludes by highlighting the implications of the rise of ISIS and the collapse of Al-Qaeda's influence for policymakers, legislators, and the general public. It underscores the need for a comprehensive understanding of the dynamics within modern terrorist organizations driven by religious ideologies. By grasping the nuances of these organizations, policymakers can devise effective strategies to counter the threat they pose, while legislators can craft legislation that addresses the underlying causes of religious extremism.

Overall, this subchapter offers a comprehensive exploration of the rise of ISIS and the decline of Al-Qaeda's influence, providing a valuable resource for scholars, academicians, politicians, legislators, and the public interested in understanding the evolution of modern terrorist organizations and the rise of religious extremism.

Ideological Foundations of ISIS

The rise of modern terrorist organizations, driven by religious extremism, has sparked concerns across the globe. One such organization that has garnered significant attention is the Islamic State of Iraq and Syria (ISIS). Understanding the ideological foundations of ISIS is crucial in comprehending the rise and actions of this notorious group. This subchapter delves into the ideological underpinnings of ISIS, shedding light on the extremist beliefs that fuel its activities.

At its core, ISIS operates based on a distorted interpretation of Sunni Islam, blending it with elements of radical Salafism and Wahhabism. These ideologies lay the groundwork for the group's theological justifications for violence, territorial expansion, and the establishment of a self-proclaimed caliphate. By examining the ideological foundations of ISIS, scholars, academicians, politicians, legislators, and the public can gain a deeper understanding of the organization's motivations and combat its influence more effectively.

ISIS subscribes to a puritanical and rigid interpretation of Islamic texts, rejecting any modern interpretations or practices deemed impure. They believe in the concept of takfir, which allows them to label other Muslims as apostates, justifying violence against them. This ideology has fueled sectarian tensions and led to brutal attacks against Shia Muslims, Yazidis, Christians, and other religious minorities.

The group also draws inspiration from medieval Islamic empire-building and aims to resurrect the caliphate, an Islamic state governed by strict Sharia law. Their vision of a caliphate extends beyond territorial control; it encompasses a global Islamic revolution aimed at uniting all Muslims under their leadership. This ideology has attracted disenchanted individuals seeking a sense of purpose and belonging.

ISIS employs sophisticated propaganda techniques to spread its extremist ideology, using social media platforms to recruit followers and justify its acts of violence. Their messaging targets vulnerable individuals by offering a utopian vision of an Islamic state, promising empowerment, and reviving the glory of the past.

Understanding the ideological foundations of ISIS is not only essential for combating the group's influence but also for addressing the broader issue of religious extremist organizations. By studying the ideological underpinnings of such organizations, policymakers and scholars can develop effective counter-narratives, policies, and strategies to undermine their appeal and prevent further radicalization.

In conclusion, the ideological foundations of ISIS lie in a distorted interpretation of Sunni Islam, blended with radical Salafism and Wahhabism. Their puritanical beliefs, combined with the desire for a global caliphate, fuel their violent actions and recruitment efforts. By comprehending these ideological underpinnings, scholars, academicians, politicians, legislators, and the public can tackle the rise of religious extremist organizations more effectively, promoting global peace, and countering the spread of violent ideologies.

Recruitment and Propagation of ISIS' Ideology

The rise of modern terrorist organizations, particularly those driven by religious ideologies, has become a major concern for scholars, academicians, politicians, legislators, and the general public alike. In this subchapter, we delve into the recruitment and propagation strategies employed by one of the most notorious groups in recent history - the Islamic State of Iraq and Syria (ISIS). By understanding the recruitment methods and ideological dissemination employed by ISIS, we can gain valuable insights into the rise of religious extremism and the factors contributing to its appeal.

ISIS, unlike traditional terrorist organizations, has harnessed the power of the internet and social media platforms to recruit individuals from all corners of the globe. Their sophisticated recruitment efforts have successfully attracted a diverse range of individuals, including vulnerable youth, disenchanted individuals, and even professionals. Through targeted online propaganda, ISIS presents an enticing narrative that resonates with individuals seeking purpose, belonging, and a sense of identity. By exploiting socio-political grievances, they manipulate potential recruits into believing that joining their cause is a duty and a path to redemption.

Furthermore, ISIS has skillfully employed various tactics to propagate its extremist ideology. They use a combination of traditional media outlets, such as magazines and videos, and social media platforms to disseminate their message. By employing a mix of graphic violence, religious justifications, and a distorted interpretation of Islamic teachings, they aim to radicalize susceptible individuals and incite them to act on their beliefs. This subchapter explores the psychological aspects behind the effectiveness of ISIS' propaganda techniques, shedding light on how the group successfully recruits and radicalizes individuals.

Understanding the recruitment and propagation strategies employed by ISIS is of paramount importance to counteracting the rise of religious extremist organizations. By comprehending the factors that contribute to their appeal, policymakers and legislators can develop effective strategies to prevent radicalization, dismantle recruitment networks, and counter extremist narratives. Scholars and academicians can contribute by conducting further research to identify vulnerabilities within societies that make individuals susceptible to extremist ideologies. This knowledge can aid in designing targeted intervention programs and educational initiatives to combat the influence of religious extremism.

In conclusion, the recruitment and propagation of ISIS' ideology represent a significant challenge in the fight against religious extremist organizations. This subchapter provides an in-depth analysis of the strategies employed by ISIS, shedding light on the factors that contribute to their success. By understanding these recruitment and propaganda techniques, we can work towards developing effective countermeasures and fostering a more resilient society against the allure of extremist ideologies.

Territorial Expansion and Governance by ISIS

Introduction:

The rise of modern terrorist organizations has brought about a significant shift in global security dynamics. One of the most notorious groups to emerge in recent times is the Islamic State of Iraq and Syria (ISIS). This subchapter explores the territorial expansion and governance strategies employed by ISIS, shedding light on the organization's methods and motivations. By understanding the evolution of ISIS, scholars, academicians, politicians, legislators, and the general public can gain valuable insights into the rise of religious extremism and its implications for global security.

Territorial Expansion:

ISIS swiftly gained international attention by capturing vast territories in Iraq and Syria, establishing a self-proclaimed caliphate. Their territorial expansion was fueled by a combination of political instability, sectarian tensions, and a power vacuum in the region. This section delves into the strategies employed by ISIS to seize and hold territory, such as the use of guerrilla warfare tactics, exploiting local grievances, and capitalizing on social media for recruitment and propaganda.

Governance:

Once in control, ISIS sought to establish a governance system that aligned with its radical interpretation of Islamic law. This subchapter examines the organization's brutal methods of governance, including imposing strict rules and punishments, indoctrinating children through education, and implementing a sophisticated taxation system to finance their operations. It also explores the challenges faced by local populations living under ISIS rule and the implications for human rights and social stability.

Motivations and Implications:

Understanding the motivations behind ISIS's territorial expansion and governance is crucial for comprehending the rise of religious extremist organizations. This section analyzes the ideological underpinnings of ISIS, their recruitment strategies, and the allure they held for individuals seeking purpose, belonging, or revenge. Additionally, it explores the broader implications of ISIS's actions, including the threat to regional stability, refugee crises, and the emergence of lone-wolf attacks in Western countries.

Conclusion:

The territorial expansion and governance strategies employed by ISIS represent a significant development in the evolution of modern terrorist organizations. By examining the rise of religious extremist organizations like ISIS, scholars, academicians, politicians, legislators, and the general public can gain valuable insights into the factors driving such organizations and their implications for global security. This subchapter serves as a comprehensive resource for understanding the complex dynamics of territorial expansion and governance by ISIS, providing a foundation for further research and analysis in the field of terrorism studies.

Chapter 4: Analysis of Religious Extremist Organizations

Recruitment and Radicalization Processes

In the pursuit of understanding the rise of religious extremism, it is crucial to thoroughly examine the recruitment and radicalization processes employed by modern terrorist organizations. This subchapter delves into the intricate mechanisms employed by these groups to attract and mold individuals into becoming willing participants in acts of violence and terrorism.

Modern terrorist organizations, particularly those driven by religious ideologies such as Islamic extremism or Christian fundamentalism, employ sophisticated recruitment strategies to identify and target vulnerable individuals. These strategies often exploit social, economic, and political grievances, seeking to capitalize on the disillusionment and discontent that individuals may feel towards the established order. By providing a sense of belonging, purpose, and empowerment, these organizations entice individuals to join their ranks and commit acts of violence in the name of their cause.

The radicalization process is a crucial stage in the recruitment of individuals into these extremist organizations. It involves the manipulation of personal beliefs, emotions, and experiences to align them with the extremist ideology propagated by these groups. Through a combination of indoctrination, propaganda, and socialization, individuals are gradually radicalized to adopt extreme views and resort to violence as a means of achieving their goals.

Religious extremism often plays a significant role in the recruitment and radicalization processes. Terrorist organizations exploit religious narratives and symbols, distorting and weaponizing religious texts to justify their violent actions. They prey upon individuals who may already have a strong religious identity, using it as a tool to manipulate their perceptions and manipulate their commitment to the cause.

Understanding the recruitment and radicalization processes is crucial for scholars, academicians, politicians, legislators, and the general public alike. By comprehending the complex strategies employed by modern terrorist organizations, we can develop effective countermeasures to prevent the recruitment and radicalization of vulnerable individuals. This knowledge allows policymakers to design targeted interventions, educational programs, and community initiatives to address the root causes of radicalization and provide alternative pathways for individuals susceptible to extremist ideologies.

In conclusion, the recruitment and radicalization processes employed by modern terrorist organizations driven by religious extremism are crucial areas of study. By examining these processes, we can gain valuable insights into the tactics used to attract individuals to violent causes and develop effective strategies to counter them. It is essential for scholars, academicians, politicians, legislators, and the general public to engage in a comprehensive understanding of these processes to safeguard our societies against the threat of religiously motivated extremism.

Financing and Support Networks

In the complex world of modern terrorist organizations, understanding the intricate web of financing and support networks is crucial to comprehending their rise and sustained existence. This subchapter delves into the intricate dynamics of how these organizations secure and manage their funds, as well as the networks that sustain their operations.

Terrorist organizations, particularly those driven by religious extremism, rely on diverse sources of funding. These range from state sponsors with their own geopolitical agendas to illicit activities such as drug trafficking, kidnapping for ransom, and money laundering. Understanding these financial channels is essential for policymakers, scholars, and legislators to disrupt and dismantle such networks effectively.

This subchapter also explores the support networks that sustain these organizations. Religious extremist organizations, including those rooted in Islamic extremism or Christian fundamentalism, thrive on the support of like-minded individuals, communities, and sympathetic entities. These networks provide ideological, logistical, and operational support, including recruitment, training, and safe havens. By understanding how these networks function and how they interact with the broader society, policymakers can develop effective countermeasures to combat their influence.

Moreover, this subchapter examines the role of the internet and social media platforms in the financing and support networks of modern terrorist organizations. The use of these platforms for propaganda, recruitment, and fundraising has become increasingly prevalent. Academicians, scholars, and the public in general must stay informed about the evolving methods employed by these organizations to exploit online platforms and ensure countermeasures are continually updated.

The content of this subchapter is invaluable for scholars and academicians seeking a comprehensive understanding of modern terrorist organizations and religious extremist movements. It also provides insight for politicians, legislators, and policymakers who play a crucial role in devising effective strategies to counter the rise of these organizations. By shedding light on the financing and support networks that sustain these organizations, this subchapter equips its readers with the knowledge needed to address this global security challenge.

In conclusion, the subchapter "Financing and Support Networks" is a vital addition to the book "The Evolution of Modern Terrorist Organizations: Understanding the Rise of Religious Extremism." It addresses the interests of scholars, academicians, politicians, legislators, and the public at large, providing valuable insights into the complex dynamics of financing and support networks that enable the growth and sustenance of modern terrorist organizations driven by religious extremism.

Use of Propaganda and Social Media

In today's digital age, the use of propaganda and social media has become an integral part of the strategies employed by modern terrorist organizations. This subchapter explores how these organizations harness the power of propaganda and social media to spread their message, recruit new members, and incite violence.

Propaganda has long been utilized by terrorist groups as a tool to manipulate public opinion and advance their ideological agenda. However, the emergence of social media platforms in recent years has provided these organizations with a powerful and unprecedented means to disseminate propaganda on a global scale. Through platforms such as Facebook, Twitter, and YouTube, terrorists can reach a vast audience instantaneously, transcending geographical boundaries and cultural barriers.

One of the key advantages of using social media for propaganda purposes is its ability to create a sense of community and belonging among potential recruits. Terrorist organizations often exploit vulnerable individuals who may feel marginalized or disconnected from society, offering them a sense of purpose and identity through their extremist ideologies. By leveraging social media platforms, these groups can establish virtual networks that foster a sense of camaraderie and belonging, making recruitment efforts more effective.

Additionally, social media allows terrorist organizations to tailor their messages to specific target audiences. Through data analytics and algorithms, they can identify individuals who may be receptive to their ideology and customize content accordingly. This personalized approach increases the likelihood of engaging potential recruits and radicalizing them further.

Furthermore, the visual and emotive nature of social media enables terrorists to craft compelling narratives that resonate with their target audience. They can present themselves as freedom fighters, martyrs, or champions of a particular cause, appealing to individuals who may feel disenchanted or disenfranchised. Through carefully curated videos, images, and stories, terrorist organizations can evoke strong emotions and instill a sense of urgency, thus motivating individuals to take action.

While the use of propaganda and social media by modern terrorist organizations poses significant challenges for governments and counter-terrorism efforts, it also presents opportunities for proactive intervention. By understanding the mechanics behind propaganda dissemination on social media, scholars, academicians, politicians, legislators, and the general public can develop effective counter-narratives to challenge extremist ideologies and disrupt recruitment efforts. Moreover, cooperation between governments, social media companies, and civil society organizations is essential to develop strategies that mitigate the spread of terrorist propaganda while safeguarding freedom of expression and privacy.

In conclusion, the use of propaganda and social media by modern terrorist organizations has revolutionized how these groups operate and communicate. The power of social media allows them to reach a wide audience, recruit new members, and incite violence more effectively than ever before. Understanding this phenomenon is crucial for scholars, academicians, politicians, legislators, and the general public in order to develop effective strategies to counter religious extremist organizations and prevent the rise of religiously motivated terrorism.

Role of Leadership in Religious Extremist Organizations

In the ever-evolving landscape of modern terrorist organizations, it is crucial to understand the role of leadership in driving religious extremism. This subchapter aims to shed light on the complex dynamics within such organizations, examining their structure, strategies, and the pivotal role leaders play in shaping their ideologies and actions.

Leadership within religious extremist organizations holds immense power and influence over their followers. These leaders often possess charismatic qualities that allow them to attract and mobilize individuals towards their cause. They exploit religious beliefs and manipulate theological interpretations to create a sense of righteousness and moral superiority among their followers. By doing so, they provide a justification for violence and radical actions, convincing their recruits to commit acts of terror in the name of their religious beliefs.

The leaders of these organizations also play a significant role in shaping the group's ideology and objectives. They interpret religious texts and selectively choose verses that align with their extremist views, distorting the original teachings to suit their violent agenda. Through charismatic speeches, propaganda, and indoctrination, they convince their followers that their cause is not only just but divinely ordained.

Furthermore, leadership in religious extremist organizations acts as a unifying force, providing strategic direction and operational guidance. They oversee the recruitment process, selecting individuals who are vulnerable, disillusioned, or seeking purpose in life. Once recruited, these individuals are subjected to intense training and ideological indoctrination, ensuring their complete allegiance to the organization and its leaders.

Leadership within religious extremist organizations is also tasked with maintaining discipline and loyalty among their followers. They establish strict hierarchies and enforce a culture of obedience, punishing any dissent or disloyalty severely. By doing so, they ensure the organization's survival and its ability to carry out acts of terror.

Understanding the role of leadership in religious extremist organizations is essential for scholars, academicians, politicians, legislators, and the public at large. It allows us to comprehend the mechanisms that drive these organizations, their strategies for recruitment and radicalization, and their potential for violence and destabilization. By gaining insights into the leadership dynamics, we can develop effective countermeasures to combat the rise of religious extremism and safeguard our societies.

In conclusion, leadership plays a pivotal role in religious extremist organizations, driving their ideologies, strategies, and recruitment processes. These leaders exploit religious beliefs, manipulate theological interpretations, and employ charismatic tactics to attract and radicalize individuals. By understanding the role of leadership, we can better address the challenges posed by modern terrorist organizations driven by religious extremism and work towards a more peaceful and inclusive future.

Impact of Religious Extremist Organizations on Global Security

Title: Impact of Religious Extremist Organizations on Global Security

Introduction:

The rise of religious extremist organizations in contemporary times has posed significant challenges to global security. This subchapter aims to shed light on the profound impact these organizations have on international stability, delving into the intricacies of modern terrorist organizations and examining their religious motivations. By understanding the roots and consequences of religious extremism, scholars, academicians, politicians, legislators, and the general public can formulate informed strategies to counter this growing threat.

Understanding Modern Terrorist Organizations:

Modern terrorist organizations have evolved in complexity and scope, employing sophisticated tactics with global reach. While political ideologies have historically fueled terrorism, the rise of religious extremism has introduced a new paradigm. These organizations, driven by religious ideologies, such as Islamic extremism or Christian fundamentalism, have become key actors in shaping global security dynamics.

Religious Extremist Organizations: Catalysts of Insecurity:

Religious extremist organizations pose multifaceted threats to global security. Firstly, their ability to recruit and radicalize individuals from diverse backgrounds has resulted in an increased number of homegrown terrorists. This phenomenon amplifies the challenge faced by security agencies, as potential threats emerge from within local communities.

Secondly, the transnational nature of these organizations enables them to forge alliances, share resources, and coordinate attacks across borders. This interconnectedness poses a significant hurdle for national security apparatuses, necessitating international cooperation to effectively combat these groups.

Furthermore, religious extremist organizations exploit societal fault lines, exacerbating existing conflicts and fueling sectarian violence. Their actions often result in destabilization of entire regions, fostering an environment conducive to the rise of further extremist groups.

Implications for Global Security:

The impact of religious extremist organizations on global security cannot be overstated. Their ability to carry out large-scale attacks, such as the events of 9/11 or the Paris attacks, create an atmosphere of fear and insecurity on a global scale. The resulting erosion of public trust and the disruption of international order have far-reaching consequences for political, economic, and social stability.

Moreover, these organizations exploit technological advancements, utilizing social media platforms to disseminate propaganda, recruit new members, and coordinate attacks. This cyber dimension adds an additional layer of complexity to countering their activities, necessitating innovative approaches to combat their online presence.

Conclusion:

Religious extremist organizations driven by ideologies have emerged as a significant threat to global security. The consequences of their actions ripple across societies, affecting political, economic, and social landscapes. By comprehending the impact of these organizations, scholars, academicians, politicians, legislators, and the general public can work collaboratively to develop effective strategies to counter religious extremism and ensure a safer future for all.

Chapter 5: Counterterrorism Strategies and Responses

International Cooperation and Collaboration

In the ever-changing global landscape, the rise of modern terrorist organizations has posed unprecedented challenges to the international community. As scholars and academicians, it is imperative to delve into the complex realm of international cooperation and collaboration in order to understand and counter the growing threat of religious extremist organizations. This subchapter aims to shed light on the significance of international cooperation in combating terrorism while exploring the unique characteristics of modern terrorist organizations driven by religious ideologies.

Modern terrorist organizations have transcended borders, harnessing the power of globalization to spread their radical ideologies and execute acts of violence. To effectively combat this menace, international cooperation becomes a crucial pillar in the fight against terrorism. Through the exchange of intelligence, sharing of best practices, and joint operations, nations can pool their resources and expertise to disrupt and dismantle these organizations. This collaborative approach not only enhances the effectiveness of counterterrorism efforts but also fosters a sense of unity and solidarity among nations in the face of a common enemy.

Religious extremist organizations, such as those driven by Islamic extremism or Christian fundamentalism, pose unique challenges due to their ideological nature. Understanding the motivations, beliefs, and strategies of these groups is essential to developing effective counterterrorism policies. International collaboration in this regard allows for the sharing of knowledge and research, enabling scholars and academicians to gain a comprehensive understanding of the complex dynamics underlying religious extremism. By examining case studies and analyzing historical trends, policymakers and legislators can formulate evidence-based strategies to address the root causes of religious radicalization and prevent the emergence of future extremist organizations.

Moreover, international cooperation facilitates the identification and disruption of the financing networks that sustain these terrorist organizations. By working together to track and cut off funding sources, nations can economically cripple these groups, significantly impeding their ability to carry out attacks. Additionally, collaboration in law enforcement and border control enables nations to effectively monitor and prevent the movement of individuals and resources across borders, reducing the risk of terrorist infiltration.

To engage the public in general, it is essential to promote awareness and understanding of the complexities surrounding modern terrorist organizations and religious extremism. By disseminating accurate information through public campaigns, educational programs, and media platforms, a wider audience can grasp the multifaceted nature of this global challenge. This knowledge empowers individuals to recognize the signs of radicalization, report suspicious activities, and contribute to the overall security of their communities.

In conclusion, international cooperation and collaboration play a pivotal role in countering the rise of modern terrorist organizations driven by religious extremism. By fostering unity among nations, sharing intelligence, and developing evidence-based strategies, policymakers, legislators, and scholars can work together to disrupt these organizations, address the root causes of radicalization, and promote global security. It is through collective efforts that we can strive towards a safer and more peaceful world, free from the grip of religious extremist ideologies.

Legal Frameworks and Legislative Measures

In the face of rising religious extremism and the emergence of modern terrorist organizations, it is crucial for societies to develop robust legal frameworks and legislative measures to effectively combat this global threat. This subchapter delves into the significance of legal frameworks and legislative measures in addressing the rise of religious extremist organizations, such as those driven by Islamic extremism or Christian fundamentalism.

Scholars, academicians, politicians, legislators, and the public in general must recognize the importance of establishing comprehensive legal frameworks that encompass both national and international dimensions. These frameworks should focus on preventive measures, intelligence gathering, prosecution, and rehabilitation programs. By doing so, states can effectively disrupt the operational capabilities of these organizations and deter potential recruits from joining their ranks.

One of the primary aims of these legal frameworks is to empower law enforcement agencies to proactively identify and disrupt the activities of modern terrorist organizations. This can be achieved through enhanced intelligence gathering, surveillance, and cooperation among national and international security agencies. Moreover, these frameworks should provide legal provisions for the prosecution of individuals involved in planning, financing, or executing terrorist acts.

Legislative measures should also address the root causes of religious extremism by promoting social inclusion, interfaith dialogue, and religious tolerance. By nurturing an environment that respects diversity and religious freedom, societies can counter the ideological appeal of extremist organizations. Additionally, rehabilitation programs should be established to reintegrate individuals who have been radicalized and provide them with opportunities to reintegrate into mainstream society.

International cooperation is paramount in addressing the transnational nature of modern terrorist organizations. States must work together to share intelligence, coordinate efforts, and harmonize their legal frameworks to ensure that terrorists do not find safe havens in different jurisdictions. This collaboration should extend to financial institutions, as states need to adopt legislation to track and disrupt the funding mechanisms that sustain these organizations.

In conclusion, the evolution of modern terrorist organizations driven by religious extremism necessitates the development of comprehensive legal frameworks and legislative measures. This subchapter emphasizes the importance of preventive measures, intelligence gathering, prosecution, and rehabilitation programs. It underscores the significance of international cooperation, social inclusion, and interfaith dialogue in countering the rise of religious extremist organizations. By adopting and implementing these legal frameworks and legislative measures, societies can effectively combat the threat posed by modern terrorist organizations and foster a more secure and inclusive world.

Intelligence and Surveillance Techniques

In the ever-evolving landscape of modern terrorist organizations, intelligence and surveillance techniques play a crucial role in understanding and countering the rise of religious extremism. This subchapter aims to provide scholars, academicians, politicians, legislators, and the public in general with an in-depth analysis of the methods employed by such organizations, specifically those driven by religious ideologies such as Islamic extremism or Christian fundamentalism.

Intelligence gathering is the backbone of any successful counterterrorism strategy. It involves collecting, analyzing, and interpreting information to identify and understand the intentions, capabilities, and vulnerabilities of terrorist organizations. Through the use of various sources, including human intelligence, signals intelligence, and open-source intelligence, intelligence agencies can paint a comprehensive picture of the activities and networks of these extremist groups.

Surveillance techniques go hand in hand with intelligence gathering, providing valuable insights into the day-to-day operations of terrorist organizations. From traditional methods like physical surveillance and wiretapping to advanced technologies such as drones, satellite imagery, and cyber surveillance, these techniques offer a means to monitor the movements, communications, and planning activities of religious extremist organizations.

However, counterterrorism efforts must strike a delicate balance between intelligence gathering and the protection of civil liberties. The use of surveillance techniques must be conducted within the framework of legal and ethical guidelines to avoid encroaching on individuals' privacy rights. Striking this balance is a challenge that requires constant reassessment and adaptation as technology and the threat landscape continue to evolve.

This subchapter will delve into case studies, highlighting successful intelligence and surveillance operations against modern terrorist organizations driven by religious extremism. It will explore the lessons learned, best practices, and the role of international cooperation in sharing intelligence and surveillance information. Understanding the methodologies employed by these groups is essential not only for academics and scholars seeking to comprehend the rise of religious extremism but also for policymakers and legislators in formulating effective counterterrorism strategies.

By examining the intelligence and surveillance techniques used to combat religious extremist organizations, this subchapter aims to contribute to a broader understanding of the evolving nature of modern terrorism. It is imperative that scholars, academicians, politicians, legislators, and the public in general appreciate the significance of intelligence gathering and surveillance in countering the threat posed by these organizations. Only through a comprehensive understanding of their ideologies, networks, and tactics can we hope to effectively combat the rise of religious extremism and safeguard our societies.

Military Interventions and Counterinsurgency Operations

In the pursuit of tackling modern terrorist organizations driven by religious extremism, military interventions and counterinsurgency operations have become integral components of national security strategies. This subchapter aims to shed light on the evolving nature of these interventions and operations, exploring their effectiveness, challenges, and potential consequences.

Military interventions involve the deployment of armed forces into foreign territories to disrupt or dismantle terrorist organizations. These interventions are often driven by the need to address immediate security threats posed by extremist groups. However, they also carry long-term implications and complexities that demand careful consideration. Scholars, academicians, politicians, legislators, and the public should engage in a comprehensive analysis of the motivations, justifications, and outcomes of such interventions.

Counterinsurgency operations, on the other hand, focus on neutralizing the influence and capabilities of terrorist organizations within a nation's own borders. These operations require a multi-faceted approach, combining military force with political, social, and economic strategies. Understanding the intricacies of counterinsurgency is crucial for scholars and policymakers, as it allows for the development of effective strategies that minimize civilian casualties and strengthen societal resilience.

One key challenge in military interventions and counterinsurgency operations lies in the balance between security and the protection of human rights. The fight against terrorist organizations should never compromise fundamental democratic values, and it is the responsibility of scholars and lawmakers to ensure that military actions adhere to international norms and standards.

Moreover, the subchapter will delve into the consequences of military interventions and counterinsurgency operations. While these operations may succeed in dismantling specific terrorist organizations, they can inadvertently contribute to the radicalization and recruitment of new extremist groups. Understanding these unintended consequences is crucial for scholars and policymakers to refine their approaches and minimize the long-term repercussions.

By examining case studies and lessons learned from past military interventions and counterinsurgency operations, this subchapter aims to provide a comprehensive understanding of their complexities and potential impacts. As scholars, academicians, politicians, legislators, and the general public, it is our collective responsibility to critically analyze these approaches and contribute to the development of more effective and sustainable strategies to combat modern terrorist organizations driven by religious extremism.

This subchapter will be of particular interest to those interested in the study of modern terrorist organizations and religious extremist organizations, such as Islamic extremism or Christian fundamentalism. It will serve as a valuable resource for scholars and academicians seeking to deepen their understanding of the evolving nature of terrorism and the challenges associated with countering it. Additionally, policymakers and legislators will find insights that can inform the development of effective counterterrorism policies and strategies.

Addressing Root Causes of Religious Extremism

Religious extremism has emerged as a significant global concern in recent years, with various terrorist organizations claiming religious justifications for their violent acts. In order to effectively combat this growing threat, it is crucial to understand the root causes that drive individuals towards religious extremism. This subchapter aims to delve into the underlying factors that contribute to the rise of religious extremist organizations, such as Islamic extremism and Christian fundamentalism, and propose strategies to address these causes.

One of the key factors leading to religious extremism is socio-economic marginalization. Many individuals who join extremist organizations come from impoverished backgrounds, feeling alienated and excluded from mainstream society. Addressing this issue requires a multi-faceted approach, including providing better educational opportunities, creating job prospects, and fostering social inclusion. By empowering marginalized communities, we can reduce the appeal of extremist ideologies and create an environment of hope and opportunity.

Another factor that drives religious extremism is the spread of extremist ideologies through online platforms. The internet has provided a breeding ground for radicalization, allowing individuals to access propaganda, connect with like-minded individuals, and plan attacks. To counter this, policymakers and tech companies need to collaborate in developing effective strategies to monitor and counter extremist content online. Additionally, promoting critical thinking and media literacy among the general public can help individuals recognize and reject extremist narratives.

A lack of religious tolerance and interfaith dialogue also contributes to the growth of religious extremism. By promoting respect and understanding among different religious communities, we can foster an environment of coexistence and mutual respect. Interfaith dialogue initiatives, educational programs, and community outreach can play a crucial role in bridging divides and promoting a culture of acceptance.

Furthermore, it is essential to address geopolitical factors that fuel religious extremism. Conflicts, political instability, and foreign interventions often provide fertile ground for extremist organizations to recruit and thrive. Engaging in diplomacy, promoting peaceful conflict resolution, and addressing the root causes of conflicts can help alleviate the grievances that extremists exploit.

In conclusion, addressing the root causes of religious extremism requires a comprehensive and multi-dimensional approach. By tackling socio-economic marginalization, countering online radicalization, promoting religious tolerance, and addressing geopolitical factors, we can undermine the appeal of extremist ideologies. This subchapter aims to provide insights and strategies to scholars, academicians, politicians, legislators, and the general public in understanding and combating the rise of religious extremism in modern terrorist organizations. It is only by addressing these root causes that we can hope to create a more peaceful and harmonious world.

Chapter 6: The Future of Modern Terrorist Organizations

Evolution of Tactics and Technologies

In the ever-evolving landscape of modern terrorist organizations, understanding the dynamics of their tactics and technologies is crucial in effectively combating the rise of religious extremism. This subchapter explores the multifaceted nature of these organizations, their adaptive strategies, and the technologies they employ to further their ideological agendas.

Terrorist organizations have, over the years, transformed their tactics to exploit vulnerabilities in society and exert maximum impact. The traditional methods of attacks, such as bombings and hijackings, have given way to more sophisticated strategies. Today, we witness the emergence of lone-wolf attacks, cyber terrorism, and the weaponization of social media platforms. These new tactics reflect the adaptability and resilience of modern terrorist organizations. Their ability to swiftly adapt to changing circumstances poses a significant challenge to security forces and intelligence agencies worldwide.

Technological advancements have played a pivotal role in the evolution of terrorist organizations. The widespread availability of the internet and social media platforms has provided them with an unprecedented means to disseminate propaganda, recruit followers, and coordinate attacks. Through the exploitation of encrypted messaging applications and the dark web, these organizations can operate in the shadows, making it difficult for law enforcement agencies to track their activities.

Furthermore, the advent of emerging technologies, such as drones and artificial intelligence, has opened up new avenues for terrorist organizations to carry out attacks. Drones have become a powerful tool for surveilling potential targets and delivering explosives, while artificial intelligence enables them to analyze vast amounts of data and identify vulnerabilities in security systems.

To effectively counter these evolving tactics and technologies, policymakers, security agencies, and scholars must stay ahead of the curve. By closely monitoring the strategies employed by terrorist organizations, we can identify patterns and develop proactive measures to prevent future attacks. Collaboration between academia, law enforcement, and technology experts is essential to understand the nuances of these organizations and devise effective countermeasures.

In conclusion, the evolution of tactics and technologies within modern terrorist organizations is a topic of utmost importance for scholars, academicians, politicians, legislators, and the public at large. Through a comprehensive understanding of the ever-changing landscape, we can work towards developing strategies that effectively dismantle the networks of religious extremist organizations. By examining the tactics and technologies employed by these organizations, we can proactively combat the rise of religious extremism and ensure a safer future for all.

Potential Threats from Emerging Religious Extremist Organizations

Religious extremism has emerged as a significant threat to global peace and security in recent decades. As the world witnesses the rise of various religious extremist organizations, it becomes crucial to understand the potential threats they pose. This subchapter aims to shed light on the dangers posed by these organizations, focusing on modern terrorist organizations driven by religious ideologies, such as Islamic extremism or Christian fundamentalism.

One of the primary threats posed by emerging religious extremist organizations is the potential for large-scale violence and terrorism. These groups often employ radical methods to advance their religious and political agendas. Their activities range from suicide bombings, kidnappings, and assassinations to mass shootings and bombings. The devastating attacks carried out by organizations like Al-Qaeda, ISIS, and Boko Haram serve as harrowing examples of the destructive capabilities of religious extremist groups.

Moreover, these organizations target vulnerable individuals, particularly the youth, who may be susceptible to their radical ideologies. Through sophisticated recruitment tactics, they lure young individuals into their ranks, indoctrinating them with extremist beliefs and grooming them to become radicalized and carry out acts of violence. This recruitment process poses a severe threat, as it allows these organizations to expand their reach and influence, potentially leading to an increase in terrorist activities.

Another concern related to religious extremist organizations is the potential for destabilizing entire regions. These groups often seek to establish their version of an ideal religious state, disregarding the sovereignty and stability of nations. Their activities can lead to violent conflicts, civil wars, and social unrest, exacerbating existing tensions within societies. This can result in mass displacement of populations, economic instability, and political turmoil, creating a fertile ground for further extremist ideologies to take root.

Furthermore, emerging religious extremist organizations have shown adaptability and resilience in the face of counterterrorism efforts. They utilize modern technology, including social media platforms, to propagate their ideologies and recruit new members. Their ability to exploit the internet for radicalization and communication poses a significant challenge for law enforcement agencies and policymakers.

To effectively counter these threats, scholars, academicians, politicians, legislators, and the public need to develop a comprehensive understanding of the motivations, strategies, and dynamics of religious extremist organizations. By analyzing case studies, studying the root causes of radicalization, and closely monitoring emerging trends, we can work towards formulating effective counterterrorism policies and strategies.

In conclusion, the emergence of religious extremist organizations presents a significant threat to global security. Their potential for violence, recruitment tactics, destabilization of regions, and adaptability pose challenges that require urgent attention. By addressing these threats through informed research, dialogue, and collaborative efforts, we can strive towards a more peaceful and secure world.

Strategies for Preventing the Rise of New Extremist Movements

In recent years, the world has witnessed the alarming rise of new extremist movements driven by religious ideologies. These organizations, such as Islamic extremism or Christian fundamentalism, pose significant challenges to global security, stability, and peace. To effectively counter this threat, it is crucial for scholars, academicians, politicians, legislators, and the general public to understand the strategies that can be employed to prevent the emergence and growth of such extremist movements.

1. Promote Education and Critical Thinking: One of the most effective long-term strategies is to invest in education and promote critical thinking. By providing quality education that emphasizes inclusivity, tolerance, and respect for diverse perspectives, societies can empower individuals to question extremist narratives and ideologies. This can help undermine the appeal of extremist movements and prevent radicalization.

2. Strengthen Community Resilience: Building strong and resilient communities is essential to prevent the rise of extremist movements. Governments, civil society organizations, and religious leaders should work together to foster social cohesion, promote dialogue, and address

grievances that could potentially fuel radicalization. Encouraging interfaith and intercultural dialogues can help bridge divides and promote understanding.

3. Counter Online Radicalization: Given the increasing influence of the internet and social media platforms, efforts to counter online radicalization are crucial. Governments and tech companies should collaborate to develop effective strategies for monitoring and removing extremist content. Promoting counter-narratives that challenge extremist ideologies can also play a vital role in preventing individuals from being swayed by extremist propaganda.

4. Address Socioeconomic Factors: Socioeconomic disparities and marginalization often create fertile ground for the growth of extremist movements. Governments should focus on addressing these root causes by implementing inclusive economic policies, reducing inequality, and providing opportunities for marginalized communities. This can help alleviate grievances that extremists exploit to recruit new members.

5. Strengthen International Cooperation: The fight against extremist movements requires international collaboration. Governments and international organizations should share intelligence, coordinate efforts, and develop joint strategies to prevent the cross-border spread of extremist ideologies. By working together, nations can effectively disrupt the financing, recruitment, and operational capabilities of these organizations.

Preventing the rise of new extremist movements is a complex and multifaceted task that requires a comprehensive approach. By implementing these strategies, scholars, academicians, politicians, legislators, and the public can contribute to countering the threat of modern terrorist organizations and religious extremist movements. It is through collective efforts that we can create a safer and more peaceful world for all.

Balancing Security Measures with Civil Liberties

In the fight against modern terrorist organizations driven by religious extremism, societies face the daunting challenge of striking a delicate balance between ensuring national security and safeguarding civil liberties. This subchapter delves into the complex task of harmonizing these two seemingly contradictory elements in the context of the evolution of modern terrorist organizations.

As scholars, academicians, politicians, legislators, and the general public, we must recognize the fundamental importance of both security measures and civil liberties. While security measures aim to protect citizens from potential harm, civil liberties form the bedrock of a democratic society, ensuring individual freedoms and rights. However, the rise of religious extremist organizations has tested the limits of this delicate equilibrium.

To effectively combat these threats, governments worldwide have implemented various security measures, including surveillance programs, intelligence sharing agreements, and enhanced border controls. While these measures have undoubtedly contributed to disrupting terrorist plots and dismantling extremist networks, they also raise concerns about the potential erosion of civil liberties. This subchapter explores the inherent tensions between security measures and civil liberties, highlighting the need for a nuanced approach that preserves both.

Understanding the evolving nature of modern terrorist organizations is crucial in this discussion. By examining the ideologies that drive them – such as Islamic extremism or Christian fundamentalism – we can analyze their impact on civil liberties. Religious extremist organizations often exploit societal vulnerabilities and grievances, exploiting their followers' religious beliefs to justify their violent actions. This necessitates a careful examination of the balance between maintaining security and respecting the religious freedom and rights of individuals.

The subchapter further explores the measures undertaken by governments to strike this balance. It delves into the legal frameworks, such as anti-terrorism legislation and intelligence gathering protocols, that seek to protect against terrorist threats while upholding civil liberties. It also examines the role of oversight bodies and judicial processes in ensuring accountability and preventing abuses of power.

Ultimately, this subchapter aims to provoke thoughtful discussions among scholars, academicians, politicians, legislators, and the general public about the intricate relationship between security measures and civil liberties. By understanding this delicate balance, we can navigate the challenges posed by modern terrorist organizations without compromising the very democratic principles we seek to protect.

Chapter 7: Conclusion

Recap of Key Findings and Insights

In this subchapter, we will recapitulate the key findings and insights discussed throughout the book "The Evolution of Modern Terrorist Organizations: Understanding the Rise of Religious Extremism." This comprehensive study aims to provide scholars, academicians, politicians, legislators, and the general public with a deep understanding of modern terrorist organizations and the rise of religious extremism, particularly in the context of Islamic extremism and Christian fundamentalism.

Throughout the book, we have explored various aspects and dimensions of modern terrorist organizations. We have analyzed the historical evolution of these organizations, tracing their roots from political ideologies to the incorporation of religious elements. By delving into case studies and examining real-life examples, we have shed light on the motivations, recruitment strategies, and operational tactics employed by these organizations.

One of the key findings of this research is the complex interplay between socio-political factors and religious ideologies that contribute to the rise of religious extremist organizations. We have identified socioeconomic grievances, political instability, and the polarization of societies as significant catalysts in the recruitment and radicalization processes. Additionally, the manipulation of religious doctrines by charismatic leaders and the exploitation of grievances have played a crucial role in attracting vulnerable individuals towards radical ideologies.

Another important insight that emerged from our analysis is the transnational nature of modern terrorist organizations. We have witnessed how these groups transcend national borders, establishing global networks that enable them to recruit, train, and carry out attacks across different regions. This interconnectedness poses a significant challenge to counter-terrorism efforts, necessitating international cooperation and intelligence sharing among nations.

Furthermore, our research highlights the importance of countering extremist narratives through comprehensive and multi-dimensional approaches. We have emphasized the significance of addressing root causes, such as socioeconomic disparities and political grievances, to prevent the radicalization of individuals. Additionally, promoting religious tolerance, empowering moderate voices within religious communities, and using targeted counter-messaging strategies have proven effective in undermining the appeal of extremist ideologies.

In conclusion, "The Evolution of Modern Terrorist Organizations: Understanding the Rise of Religious Extremism" provides a comprehensive examination of the factors driving the emergence and sustenance of religious extremist organizations. By analyzing key findings and insights, we have underscored the need for a holistic approach that addresses both the socio-political factors and religious ideologies that fuel radicalization. This book serves as a valuable resource for scholars, academicians, politicians, legislators, and the general public interested in understanding and combating the menace of modern terrorist organizations and religious extremism.

Implications for Scholars, Academicians, and Policymakers

In the ever-evolving landscape of modern terrorism, it is crucial for scholars, academicians, and policymakers to stay abreast of the implications that arise from the rise of religious extremism within terrorist organizations. The book, "The Evolution of Modern Terrorist Organizations: Understanding the Rise of Religious Extremism," delves deep into this subject matter, providing a comprehensive analysis that will be of immense value to individuals across various domains. This subchapter specifically focuses on the implications for scholars, academicians, and policymakers, shedding light on the significance of their roles in combating religious extremist organizations.

For scholars and academicians, this subchapter serves as an invaluable resource, offering a wealth of knowledge and insights into the intricacies of modern terrorist organizations. By exploring the origins, motivations, and tactics employed by these groups, scholars can gain a deeper understanding of the complex dynamics at play. This knowledge can inform their research, allowing them to contribute to the growing body of literature on terrorism and religious extremism. Additionally, it enables scholars to identify emerging trends and patterns, providing a basis for the development of effective counterterrorism strategies.

Policymakers and legislators play a crucial role in shaping national security and counterterrorism policies. Understanding the implications of religious extremist organizations is paramount for them to create laws and regulations that can effectively address the threat. This subchapter provides policymakers with a comprehensive overview of the challenges posed by these groups, enabling them to craft evidence-based policies that safeguard the interests of their nations. By recognizing the underlying factors that contribute to the rise of religious extremism, policymakers can develop strategies that address root causes, such as social exclusion, economic disparities, and political grievances.

For the general public, this subchapter offers a unique opportunity to gain insight into the workings of modern terrorist organizations driven by religious ideologies. By enhancing their understanding, individuals can actively engage in discussions around terrorism and religious extremism, fostering a more informed and empathetic society. This knowledge empowers the public to challenge stereotypes, promote dialogue, and support initiatives aimed at countering the allure of religious extremism.

In conclusion, the implications outlined in this subchapter hold immense significance for scholars, academicians, policymakers, legislators, and the general public. By comprehending the complexities of modern terrorist organizations driven by religious extremism, stakeholders can contribute to the development of effective counterterrorism strategies, foster dialogue, and ultimately work towards curbing the rise of such organizations.

Final Thoughts on the Evolution of Modern Terrorist Organizations

In this subchapter, we delve into the culmination of our exploration, shedding light on the evolution of modern terrorist organizations. Throughout this book, we have examined the rise of religious extremism and its impact on the formation and growth of these organizations. As scholars, academicians, politicians, legislators, and the general public, it is crucial to understand the intricate dynamics and underlying factors that have contributed to the emergence of such groups.

Modern terrorist organizations have undergone a significant transformation over the years, adapting to the changing socio-political landscape and utilizing advancements in technology to further their goals. The rise of religious extremist organizations, driven by ideologies such as Islamic extremism or Christian fundamentalism, has brought forth new challenges and complexities in combating terrorism.

One key aspect to consider is the role of globalization and the interconnectedness of our world. As information and ideas spread rapidly across borders, terrorist organizations have capitalized on this phenomenon, using it to recruit, radicalize, and communicate with their followers. Understanding the global reach and influence of these organizations is essential in formulating effective counter-terrorism strategies.

Additionally, the evolution of modern terrorist organizations has been fueled by factors such as socio-economic disparities, political grievances, and the erosion of trust in governmental institutions. Religious extremism often finds fertile ground in societies plagued by these issues, exploiting the vulnerabilities of marginalized populations and offering them a sense of identity, purpose, and belonging.

Furthermore, the use of social media and the internet has revolutionized the way terrorist organizations operate. Online platforms have become breeding grounds for radicalization, propaganda dissemination, and recruitment. The power of online networks cannot be underestimated, and efforts to counter extremist narratives must extend to the digital realm.

In conclusion, the evolution of modern terrorist organizations demands a comprehensive and multifaceted approach. Scholars, academicians, politicians, legislators, and the general public must recognize the complex interplay of religious extremism and socio-political factors in the formation and growth of these organizations. By understanding the underlying causes, global interconnectedness, and the role of technology, we can develop more effective counter-terrorism strategies that address the root causes of terrorism and promote peace and stability in our societies.

As we continue our collective efforts to combat religious extremist organizations, let us remain vigilant, informed, and united in our resolve to protect the values of tolerance, diversity, and respect for all. Only through a comprehensive understanding of the evolution of modern terrorist organizations can we hope to create a safer and more peaceful future for generations to come.